NOTTINGHAM PLAYHOUSE

SCENES FROM A FRIENDSHIP

BY JANE UPTON

Scenes from a Friendship was first performed at
Nottingham Playhouse on 15 May 2026.

SCENES FROM A FRIENDSHIP

BY JANE UPTON

JESS	Katie Redford
BILLY	Benedict Salter
Director	Hannah Stone
Designer	Abby Clarke
Lighting Designer	Alex Musgrave
Sound Designer and Composer	Ellie Isherwood
Movement Director	Michela Meazza
Dramaturg	Sarah Dickenson
Dialect Coach	Anita Gilbert
Artist Wellbeing Practitioner	Nikki Disney
Stage Manager	Vivi Wei

Katie Redford | Jess

Katie is an actress and writer from Nottingham.

Her acting credits include: *Can You Keep A Secret, Alma's Not Normal, Not Going Out, Casualty, Still Open All Hours, Young Hyacinth* (BBC); *Outlander* (Amazon); *Mount Pleasant* (Sky) and *Cold Call* (Channel 5).

After winning the BBC Norman Beaton Fellowship, she also works extensively in radio and has voiced characters for *The Archers* alongside many other audio dramas.

Benedict Salter | Billy

Benedict trained at LAMDA.

Theatre credits include: *The Curious Case of Benjamin Button* (West End and Southwark Playhouse); *The Score* (Theatre Royal Bath); *Othello, The Importance of Being Earnest, A Little Night Music* (Watermill Theatre); *Lone Flyer* (Jermyn Street Theatre and Hull Truck – shortlisted for Best Supporting Performance, Off-West End Awards 2022); *Lady Windermere's Fan, An Inspector Calls* (West End); *A Christmas Carol* (Derby Theatre); *Vespertilio* (VAULT Festival and Dublin Fringe); *The Last Days of Anne Boleyn* (Tower of London) and *Shakespeare in Music* (RSC/ Southbank Sinfonia).

Voice credits include: *Final Fantasy XVI: The Rising Tide* (Square Enix).

Jane Upton | Writer

Jane Upton is a playwright.

Theatre credits include: *(the) Woman* (New Perspectives/Royal & Derngate – 2025; transferred to Park Theatre, London, Autumn 2025); *The Price of Home* (Paines Plough & Derby Theatre); *Finding Nana* (New Perspectives, 2017 – 2018); *All the Little Lights* (Fifth Word – George Devine Award, 2016; UK tour 2017); *Watching the Living* (New Perspectives Theatre UK tour, 2014); *Swimming* (Menagerie Theatre Hotbed Festival, 2013; Soho/Edinburgh Festival, 2014); and *Bones* (Fifth Word – Edinburgh Festival/UK tour, 2011–2012).

She is the winner of the 2024 Off West End 'Adopt a Playwright Award' for *Belongings*, which had a rehearsed reading at the Criterion Theatre, London in 2025.

Hannah Stone | Director

Hannah Stone (she/her) is a director and theatremaker. Theatre credits include: *The King Stone* by Charlotte East (developed with support of the National Theatre Generate Programme); *Dweeb-A-Mania* by Sarah Middleton for Polka Theatre, *The Trials* (Nottingham Playhouse – ★★★★★ 'An utterly gripping and powerful production' – East Midlands Theatre); *SHEWOLVES* by Sarah Middleton (touring production including Edinburgh Fringe and Southwark Playhouse – published by Concord Theatricals); *Pinocchio* by Sarah Middleton (Nottingham Playhouse/Mercury Colchester) and *Goldilocks* by Anna Wheatley (Nottingham Playhouse).

Hannah is Co-Artistic Director of the Nottingham-based company Rebel Sparks, founded in 2011. The company have created and toured numerous shows, notably *Aidy the Awesome* (commissioned by Leicester Curve and supported by Arts Council England). Hannah was an Associate Artist at Nottingham Playhouse between 2020 and 2023.

Abby Clarke | Designer

Abby is a theatremaker and designer working across theatre, live performance and installation.

Awards include: finalist, Off West End Awards 2024 for Set Design and Costume Design; nominated for Best Designer, The Stage Debut Awards 2019; nominated for the Naomi Wilkinson Award for Stage Design; and finalist, Linbury Prize for Stage Design 2017.

Design credits include: *War of the Worlds* (imitating the dog – national and international tour); *A Symphony of Flesh and Bones* (Manchester International Festival); *All Change* (imitating the dog); *In the Ruins of the Big House* (Factory International); *Lifeline* (Southwark Playhouse); *The Jolly Christmas Postman* (Royal & Derngate); *Beauty and the Beast* (Albany Theatre); *Unfortunate* (UK tour); *Road* (Leicester Curve); *Scissorhandz* (Southwark Playhouse); *The Owl Who Came for Christmas* (Leicester Curve); *Beauty and the Beast* (Theatre by the Lake); *As You Write It* (Shakespeare North Playhouse); *The Bear Who Went to War* (regional tour); *The Show Windows* (Coventry City of Culture); *The Allesley Silas, Read All About It, In the Meantime We Try* (Belgrade Theatre); *Bird in the Window* (UK tour); *The Furies; Living Together* (Oxford Playhouse); *The Witching Way* (Royal Exchange Theatre); *Luminosity, SWIM, Our Friends in the North* (HOME); *Prince Gorge* (Camden People's Theatre); *Dia-Beat-Es* (UK tour); *HMS Pinafore* (Minack Theatre); and *Humans at Work* (Warwick Arts Centre).

Alex Musgrave | Lighting Designer

Theatre credits include: *The White Factory* and *The Wanderers* (Marylebone Theatre – Off West End Award nominations for Best Lighting Design); *You Are Here, The Soon Life, Before After* and *Romeo and Juliet* (Southwark Playhouse – Off West End Award nominations for Best Lighting Design); *The Forsyte Saga – Parts 1 & 2* (Swan Theatre, Royal Shakespeare Company and Park Theatre, Finsbury Park); *Home* (Chichester

Festival Theatre); *Ottilie, Stones in His Pockets, Sherlock and the Whitechapel Fiend, Treasure Island* and *Private Lives* (Barn Theatre, Cirencester; Salisbury Playhouse; Bolton Octagon; Everyman Theatre, Cork); *Dracula* (National Youth Theatre); *Next to Normal* (Mountview); *The Seagull: True Story, The White Rose* and *The Last Word* (Marylebone Theatre, London); *Extraordinary Women* (Jermyn Street Theatre); *Opera Shorts* (Buxton International Festival); *Figaro: An Original Musical* (London Palladium); *A Christmas Carol* (The Lowry, Manchester); *Unbound – A New Musical, A Concert* (Hoxton Hall, London); *Kin – The Musical* (Teatro Technis, London); *It's a MotherF**king Pleasure* (SoHo Playhouse, New York City; Southbank Centre; Soho Theatre, London; National and European tours); *The Cunning Little Vixen* (Royal Birmingham Conservatoire) and *Rapunzel* (The Watermill Theatre).

Alex was nominated for two Off West End Awards for Best Lighting Design and was the Association of Lighting Production and Design Lumière Awards winner in 2019.

Ellie Isherwood | Sound Designer and Composer

Ellie Isherwood is a sound designer, composer, actor/ musician and synth-pop artist (BYFYN).

Theatre credits include: *The Dark* (stage adaptation of Lemony Snicket's *The Dark*) and *Dweeb-a-mania* (Polka Theatre) as composer and sound designer; *Alice's Adventures in Wonderland* (Orange Tree Theatre); *Disco Inferno* (National Youth Theatre); *The Sleep Show* (UK tour); *Cartoonopolis* (Pleasance); *The Gel* (New Diorama); *The Intrusion* (UK tour); *Tender* (The Bush Theatre); *The Fir Tree* (Arts Depot); *Son of a Bitch* (Summerhall, Edinburgh Fringe); *The Odyssey* (The Unicorn); *The Light Princess* (The Albany, Deptford/ARC Stockton Arts Centre); *The Glass Ceiling Beneath the Stars* (Pleasance) and *Ruby Wax: I'm Not As Well As I Thought I Was* (UK tour).

This year, Ellie was made Associate Artist at The New Wolsey Theatre and was a finalist for the Stiles and Drewe Best New Song Prize for her song 'Nice Girls Never Win' from the upcoming musical *VAMP*.

Michela Meazza | Movement Director

Michela Meazza is a movement director and choreographer.

Theatre credits include: *R.O.I. (Return on Investment)* (Hampstead Theatre – dir. Chelsea Walker); *Macbeth* (Chester Storyhouse – dir. Jamie Sophia Fletcher); *The Da Vinci Code* (Salisbury Playhouse & Mercury Theatre – dir.

Chelsea Walker); *Piaf* (Watermill Theatre – dir. Kimberley Sykes); *All's Well That Ends Well* (Sam Wanamaker Playhouse – dir. Chelsea Walker); *The New Real* (RSC – dir. Holly Race Roughan); *The Lightest Element* (Hampstead Theatre – dir. Alice Hamilton) and *Visit From An Unknown Woman* (Hampstead Theatre – dir. Chelsea Walker); *This Much I Know* (Hampstead Theatre Downstairs – dir. Chelsea Walker); *Vanya* (Duke of York's Theatre – dir. Sam Yates); *The Land of Might Have Been* (Buxton International Festival – dir. Kimberley Sykes); *The Vortex* (Chichester Festival Theatre – dir. Daniel Raggett); *The Comedy of Errors* (Mercury Theatre Colchester – dir. Ryan McBryde); *Hedda Gabler* (Sherman Theatre, Cardiff – dir. Chelsea Walker); *The Phlebotomist* (dir. Sam Yates) and *Cymbeline* (Shakespeare's Globe – dir. Sam Yates).

Performer credits with Matthew Bourne's New Adventures include: *The Midnight Bell*; *The Red Shoes*; *Swan Lake*; *Cinderella*; *Dorian Gray*; *Edward Scissorhands*; *Play Without Words*; *Nutcracker!* and *The Car Man*.

Awards include: Outstanding Female Modern Performance Award, National Dance Awards 2021.

Sarah Dickenson | Dramaturg

Sarah is a playwright and dramaturg with over twenty years' experience working both nationally and internationally. In 2025 she received the Writers' Guild of Great Britain's Olwen Wymark Award for her dramaturgy, and she is also a recipient of the Playwrights' 73 Bursary, undertaking a joint placement with Exeter Northcott Theatre and Shakespeare's Globe to write a new play.

Professional roles include: Associate Dramaturg at LAMDA, Paines Plough, and the Royal Shakespeare Company; Production Dramaturg at Shakespeare's Globe; Senior Reader at Soho Theatre; Literary Manager at Theatre503 and New Writing Associate at The Red Room.

Theatre credits include: *The Commotion Time* (Exeter Northcott Theatre, 2024).

Anita Gilbert | Dialect Coach

Theatre credits include: *Punch, The Trials, The Ugly Duckling* (Nottingham Playhouse); *Larkrise to Candleford* (Watermill Theatre/ Theatre by the Lake); *Memory of Water* (Bolton Octagon); *First Encounters: Romeo & Juliet* (RSC); *Chariots of Fire, Rock/ Paper/Scissors, We Could All Be Perfect* (Sheffield Theatres) *Big Big Sky* (New Vic Stoke); *Gods Of Salford* (Lowry Theatre/Not too Tame); *Twelfth Night* (Shakespeare North Playhouse/Not Too Tame) and *Little Shop of Horrors, Oliver*

Twist, The Great Gatsby, Kiss Me Quickstep, Of Mice and Men, Welfare, Cinderella, Brassed Off, Jekyll and Hyde, Homegirl, Extra Time, Abi, What Fatima Did, One Man, Two Guvnors, Treasure Island, The Little Mermaid, 4 Walls, Mr Burns, The Wind in the Willows (Derby Theatre).

Screen & Audio credits include: *Waterloo Road* (BBC); *Witches of Essex* (Sky History); *Hollyoaks* (Lime Pictures); *Bonny Chip* (Fox & Cox Prod.) and *You Cannot Thread a Moving Needle* (BBC Radio 4 Drama).

Nikki Disney | Artist Wellbeing Practitioner

Nikki is a state registered Drama and Movement therapist and Clinical Supervisor (MA. HCPC, Badth), who has worked as an Artist Wellbeiing Practitioner for twelve years. She has implemented and delivered safeguarding, access and wellbeing procedures within arts organisations such as Nottingham Playhouse, The Royal Court and The National Theatre of Scotland; specialising in themes of trauma, mental health and autobiographical material.

She has delivered training and implemented tool kits for wellbeing in the rehearsal room. In 2025 she released a paper on creating a Trauma Informed Frameworks for productions via Theatre Topics, written with Nesrin Alrefaai.

Vivi Wei | Stage Manager

Vivi Wei is a technical and stage manager, performer and singer from China. Her roles in stage management, acting, singing and workshop facilitation span the UK and China, but her true passion lies in multi-disciplinary approaches, particularly in migrant theatre, utilising storytelling to address sociopolitical issues and amplify marginalised voices.

Her work includes: *Most Favoured* (Soho Theatre); *The Dao of Unrepresentative British Chinese Experience* (Kakilang, Soho Theatre); *Cinderella* (Brixton House); *USELESS* (Brixton House); *Arrogant Soft* (Riverside Studio); *Project Atom Boi* (Camden People's Theatre, Artist Choice Award in Vault Festival); *NOSHOW* (Park Theatre); *Lessons on Revolution* (Jermyn Street Theatre) and *Dreamaker Theatre Festival* (Changjiang Theatre, Shanghai).

Work with young people includes: *Assembly Festival* (Company Three) and *KATZENMUSIK* (London Youth Theatre).

NOTTINGHAM PLAYHOUSE

Nottingham Playhouse is one of the UK's leading producing theatres, named Theatre of the Year 2025 in The Stage Awards.

Over 70 years, they have built a legacy of bold, ambitious and diverse productions that tour nationally and internationally.

The two times Olivier Award winning *Punch* by **James Graham**, commissioned and produced by Nottingham Playhouse, and directed by Artistic Director **Adam Penford**, transferred simultaneously to London's West End and Broadway in 2025. A UK Tour in 2027 has been announced, as has a special schools version.

The 2026 season includes: the world premieres of *Scenes from a Friendship* by Jane Upton and *The Market Deeping Model Railway Club* by William Ivory and the regional premiere of Beth Steel's West End hit, *Till the Stars Come Down*.

Nottingham Playhouse empowers local communities and emerging artists through their Participation and Amplify programmes and is also a Theatre of Sanctuary.

nottinghamplayhouse.co.uk

Company Manager	Patricia Davenport
Head of Construction	Janine Forster
Lead Scenic Metalworker	Marc Barrett
Lead Scenic Carpenter	Daniel Anderson
Workshop Assistant	Alex Clarke
Head of Costume	Emilie Carter
Costume Assistant	Eloisa Roan
Head of Lighting and Video	Francois Langton
Deputy Head of Lighting and Video	Ryan Moore
Technician (Lighting)	Penny Coke-Woods
Artist Development Producer	Beccy D'Souza
Producer	Jack Hudson
Programme Coordinator	Sarah Kelly
Director of Technical and Production	Andrew Quick
Technical and Production Manager	Jamie Smith
Production Coordinator	Leila Glen
Head of Props	Hannah Zemlak
Head of Scenic Art	Claire Thompson
Deputy Head of Scenic Art	Erin Fleming
Head of Sound	Matt Sims
Deputy Head of Sound	Tom Codd
Technician (Sound)	Cameron Lloyd
Head of Stage	Tony Topping
Deputy Head of Stage	Kush Patel
Technician (Stage)	Laura Wolczyk
Apprentice Technician	Jace Daws
Apprentice Technician	James Van Aardt

Sets, Scenic Art, Costume, Props, Lighting, Sound, Video, Stage Management and Technical are made or managed by the Nottingham Playhouse team, supported by freelancers.

SCENES FROM A FRIENDSHIP

Jane Upton

Author's Note

This play is a love letter to brilliant school friends who I'm still lucky enough to know. Katie, Sukhi, Kelly, Karen and Emma – the memories are carved into me; to my big sister Katie and little brother Jonathan – best friends forever; and especially to Chris, my friend from first-year juniors and one of the greatest loves of my life.

Thanks to Adam Penford at Nottingham Playhouse for his kindness, support and encouragement. Thanks to the wise, insightful, endlessly supportive dramaturg Sarah Dickenson who makes me better and teaches me so much about myself. Thanks to director Hannah Stone for her passion, commitment, kindness and patience and for building a creative team full of brilliant and kind people. Thanks to Lizzy Watts, Lydia Fleming and Jack Quarton for their insightful work on the script, pre-rehearsals. Thanks to Katie Redford and Benedict Salter for the love, care, energy and laughter. Thanks to Fran who gives me little dopamine hits when she knows I'm dragging around in my own dirt. Thanks to Mum and Dad for their devotion and support and for loving our kids as much as we do. And thanks to Mark, for steering us through some crazy times and always coming back. Love is the best.

J.U.

'It is a joy to be hidden, and a disaster not to be found.'

DW Winnicott, Playing and Reality

For Chris

Characters

BILLY
JESS

Notes

When there's no full stop at the end of a line it usually means the other character interrupts – there's not much air when Jess and Billy are together.

Jess and Billy barely ever touch.

Some of Jess's insults in the play were rewritten during rehearsals based on casting.

On page 23: 'A ginger little John Major' can be changed to 'A moany little John Major'.

On page 28: In 'You look like Elaine Paige fucked Boris Becker…' Boris Becker can be changed to another nineties male celebrity who (however loosely) resembles the actor playing Billy.

This is a work of fiction. Any resemblance to actual persons, living or dead, is purely coincidental.

This text went to press before the end of rehearsals and so may differ slightly from the play as performed.

Scene One

Billy, Where Are You? – 2023, Forty-Three

JESS. Billy. I'm scared now. Where are you? I went to your office but they said you weren't there. I'm going half mad thinking of everything I've ever said. I wanted to get on the train but I've never seen you like that. I'm so sorry. You're right. I'm a mess. There's nothing you can say worse than what I say to myself. You're an incredible dad. You've built this incredible life. I know it's over now, I know. And I promise I'll leave you alone. But please, just let me know you're okay.

PART ONE

CHILDHOOD

Scene Two

Mortiana – 1992, Twelve

Jess's house.

BILLY. Let's toss a coin for it.

JESS. You can't be Mortiana.

BILLY. Sexist.

JESS. It's my wig.

BILLY. I haven't got nits.

JESS. It won't fit a globe. Anyway, I've got the acting experience.

BILLY. I've done some acting.

JESS. Are you talking about that Nativity video your mum showed us? Full Ian McKellen at four. DO YOU HAVE A ROOM FOR MY WIFE WITH CHILD?

BILLY. Guess that means I got the first main part though.

JESS. I didn't know you then. Doesn't count. I got the first main part.

BILLY. What was it?

JESS. Humpty Dumpty. Fuck off. I didn't even audition. They saw something in me apparently.

BILLY. Yeah, you reminded them of Humpty Dumpty.

JESS. Fuck. Off. Anyway, I got the first main part.

BILLY. Doesn't mean you get to be Mortiana.

JESS. It's my house. Mum and Dad said they're watching in twenty minutes.

BILLY. Twenty minutes?

JESS. Exactly. (*Beat.*) You're the Sheriff. Do it like Alan Rickman, don't put your own slant on it.

BILLY. Alright!

JESS. You come in the door and I'll be behind the armchair like it's my lair type thing. You have to kick the rats off the plank.

BILLY. I know.

JESS. Tell a raven to shut up

BILLY. I KNOW.

JESS. And then I'll come.

BILLY. Okay.

Ready?

JESS. Yep.

BILLY *comes in as FULL Alan Rickman, taking it very seriously.*

BILLY. Mortiana?!
    (*To the rats.*) Ugh.
    (*To the raven.*) Shut up.

    JESS *appears FULL Mortiana – the heavy breathing, the weird E.T. walk – proper going for it, holding a baking tin.*

    BILLY *starts to laugh.*

JESS. Don't laugh.

BILLY. You gonna do it like that though?

JESS. Like what? Perfect? Focus on your own acting, Eyeballs! Carry on.

BILLY (*as Alan Rickman*). Mortiana!

    JESS *goes full Mortiana again.*

    You called, Madam?

    JESS *mimes swilling blood round the baking tin.*

    They act out a few lines from Robin Hood: Prince of Thieves *before* JESS *melodramatically sees the future and screams in full character, throwing the tin to the floor.* BILLY *has to cover his whole mouth to stop himself bursting into hysterics before they both crack up laughing.*

    That's how she does it!

    Right! I'm gonna cut your heart out

BOTH. with a spoon!!!

    They're laughing.

Scene Three

Post-Show Party – 1995, Fifteen

At school.

JESS. Make way for the celebrity.

BILLY. Shut up.

I'll sign your programme if you want.

JESS. I was actually in it.

BILLY. Were you?

JESS. Fuck off.

BILLY. I can't believe it's all over.

JESS. You'll be crying yourself to sleep tonight.

BILLY. It was amazing, wasn't it?

JESS. Did you see all your ex-girlfriends in the crowd? Stunned to silence.

BILLY. That final scene, Jess! I could feel the whole audience just like

JESS. The crying part was a bit

BILLY. What?

JESS. Gazza.

BILLY. Lindsay said Miss Riley was crying

JESS. She wasn't

BILLY. How could you see Miss Riley?

JESS. Street Girl Number Three spends quite a lot of time in the wings.

BILLY. You were good.

JESS. I was the only one wearing leggings.

BILLY. I don't know why you didn't just wear the costume.

JESS. As if I'm gonna let the whole school see me in fishnets?

BILLY. Your legs aren't that bad. Honestly, you were good. When you came on I could feel

JESS. It's only a school play, Billy. Get over it.

You're gonna get big parts now.

BILLY. You will as well.

JESS. No one's gonna remember me from that.

BILLY. Year 9s are never usually in it. So you're already on the list. There'll be other plays.

JESS. My mum and dad said you were brilliant.

BILLY. Ah thanks.

JESS. Where did your mum go?

BILLY. I told her not to hang around because of the party.

JESS. It's dead. Mr Hallam on the decks is the fuck-off gravestone.

BILLY. Loads of the others have gone across to The Oak.

JESS. No one told me.

BILLY. I said we'd go.

JESS. Nah. I'm starting my Saturday job at Woolworths tomorrow.

BILLY. So what?

JESS. Anyway, I don't think the sixth-form 'street girls' like me.

BILLY. It's cos you say mean stuff when you're nervous.

JESS. It's cos I wouldn't dress up as a slag.

BILLY. Lindsay's cool though. She's different.

JESS. I don't want to sit there watching you spunking over Lindsay while dissecting every scene I wasn't in.

BILLY. Honestly, Jess /

JESS. I'm not doing another play unless I get a main part.

BILLY. Well, you won't get one by being a bitch and crying in your bed. Come on. I'll buy you a bag of pork scratchings.

JESS. Only cos I don't want to waste this make-up.

Scene Four

Coming Out – 1995, Fifteen

At a house party. BILLY *is hiding in a small room/under the stairs/toilet.*

BILLY. Jess. Quick, come in here

JESS. What you doing?

BILLY. Hiding. Marie's hammered and following me round.

JESS. Well, you might've given her the wrong idea by getting off with her last week. God, this party's lame. You can't have a house party and block off half the rooms. It's not National Trust.

BILLY. Jess. I need to tell you something.

JESS. What?

BILLY. Sit down.

JESS. Can I turn the light on?

BILLY. No. Leave it.

JESS. Is it about me?

BILLY. No.

JESS. Lindsay?

BILLY. No.

JESS. What then?

BILLY. Shut up a minute, will you.

   She tries to. She can't.

JESS. You're scaring me. You're sweating. Just tell me.

BILLY. Okay.
   I think.
   I've been thinking.
   I'm gay.

JESS. Wow. Okay.

BILLY. What?

JESS. You're not, sure though?

BILLY. I mean. I don't know. Yeah. I'm gay. I think.

JESS. Oh my God.

BILLY. What?

JESS. Marie. And Charlotte. And that girl in juniors, Rosie whatshername

BILLY. Rosie Wilson.

JESS. And Lindsay. All the shagging.

BILLY. Lindsay's a lesbian.

JESS. What?

BILLY. We've been meeting up to talk about all this.

JESS. You told me you had sex at the back of Springy Park.

BILLY. Sorry.

JESS. Dickhead. You could have told me.

BILLY. I wasn't sure.

JESS. You were always taking the piss out of Mr Hallam.

BILLY. Yeah, because everyone else was.

JESS. But you were like the worst.

BILLY. Alright.

JESS. What does Lindsay say?

BILLY. She gets it.

JESS. She's only been your friend since the school play though. I mean, you never seemed gay. Before.

BILLY. What does gay seem like?

JESS. I dunno. Elton John, Boy George. Tom Hanks in *Philadelphia*.

BILLY. Tom Hanks isn't gay.

JESS. No leading actors are gay, that's why.

BILLY. Ian McKellen?

JESS. Ian McKellen's never gonna be James Bond though, is he? Have you told your mum?

BILLY. Course not.

JESS. Don't tell anyone else. Not yet.

Beat.

Have you tried stuff?

BILLY. No.

JESS. It fucking kills.

BILLY. How do you know?

JESS. *More Magazine* did a feature on it.

You need to be careful. You've seen the adverts. Don't go shagging loads of old men in dirty toilets.

BILLY. Jesus, Jess.

JESS. I mean it.

BILLY. There's other stuff anyway. Not just

JESS. Like what?

BILLY. Lindsay's got a few gay mates. She told me about it. She's going to take me to a gay bar.

JESS. We're fifteen.

BILLY. She says *I'll* get in.

JESS. Well, don't let her talk you into it.

BILLY. She's not.

Beat.

JESS. So who do you fancy then?

BILLY. You can't tell anyone.

JESS. I won't.

BILLY. You've got to swear.

JESS. On my mum's life.

Beat.

BILLY. Ashley.

JESS. Ashley Timms?! The fittest boy in school! No way is he gay.

BILLY. Never said he was.

JESS. He's proper masculine.

BILLY. I never said he was gay, Jess. Please don't tell anyone. Honestly. He can't find out.

JESS. You used to go round there for tea in juniors. He'd go mad if he knew. Don't tell anyone anything for now.

BILLY. Lindsay said I should be honest about it.

JESS. Yeah well, she's not in Year 10 with our band of fucking nutters, is she? My sister's friends are always asking when we're going to get together.

BILLY. Ugh.

JESS. Oh right, but you'll finger Charlotte Curtis after she's pissed herself down the canal.

BILLY. Do you ever forget anything?

JESS. Nope. No. I don't.

Scene Five

Beaten-Up – 1995, Fifteen

BILLY *has called* JESS *on the home-phone landline.*

JESS. Dad. I can tell you're listening in. You sound like Fred West. Hang up.

Sound of a receiver being replaced.

Sorry. They think we're going out.

BILLY *is stifling cries.*

Billy? Are you okay?

BILLY. I got beaten up.

JESS. What? Where?

BILLY. Nottingham Road.

JESS. By who?

BILLY. Dean Allen from Year 11.

JESS. Shit. Are you okay? Where are you?

BILLY. I'm at home.

JESS. Who were you with?

BILLY. Lindsay.

JESS. What did she do?

BILLY. She ran away.

JESS. She left you?

BILLY. I don't blame her.

JESS. I do.

BILLY. He went for her as well.

JESS. Fucking Dean Allen. Dirty bastard. Stinks like skidmarks.
    What did he say?

BILLY. Nothing, just, drunk I think and, just

JESS. I'll kill him. Did he hurt you?

BILLY. A bit.

JESS. He looks like a rat in a test-tube trial. Why did he do it?

BILLY. Dunno.

JESS. Do you think, cos you were with Lindsay and

BILLY. No.

JESS. What were you wearing?

BILLY. It's not cos of

JESS. This is what I mean, Billy. This is why I said don't tell
    anyone. Because Lindsay said, and so many people know
    now.

BILLY. It wasn't that. He thought I was someone else.

JESS. Right. Sorry.

D'ya want to come round? My grandma and grandad are here but

BILLY. Nah. It's alright.

JESS. I can come to you. You haven't even given me your new address.

BILLY. It's okay. Mum's here.

JESS. I'll get Dad to drop me round.

BILLY. No. I'm fine. The house is a mess. We haven't unpacked or anything.

JESS. As if I care. I know you've moved to Scarfield Flats, Billy.

BILLY. It's not that. Honestly, I'm alright. Mum'll probably want to

JESS. What?

BILLY. Talk it through or whatever

JESS. Have you told her? That you're

BILLY. No.

JESS. What about your dad?

BILLY. I haven't seen him. He's got Cathy and his Volvo.

It's alright. I think Mum's making hot chocolate.

JESS. Okay. I'll meet you in the morning, yeah? We can walk into school together.

BILLY. Yeah.

JESS. And I swear if that little fucking mole-rat comes anywhere near you, I'll

BILLY. You'll what?

JESS. Whisper something really fucking nasty under my breath and give him the evils. Probably.

Scene Six

Section 28 – 1995, Fifteen

School. Break-time.

JESS. What did Miss Riley want?

BILLY. What?

JESS. I saw you walking out the school gate with her

BILLY. Oh. Yeah, she was just going on about me getting beaten up, asking if I'm okay. She said, 'I need you to know I'm asking this as a friend, not a teacher.'

JESS. That's weird.

BILLY. Yeah.

JESS. You are okay, aren't you.

BILLY. I'm fine.

JESS. I thought she was confessing her lesbian sex secrets.

BILLY. Nah.

    Beat.

JESS. Do you want to come round tonight? I've taped *My So-Called Life*. We can rewind all the Jared Leto scenes.

BILLY. I'm not gay, Jess.

JESS. Oh.

BILLY. I'm definitely not. I'm sorry, I think Lindsay just made me feel.

JESS. Right.

    Beat.

BILLY. I heard about you, anyway. Round the back of the bins with Byron Slater. What was that all about?

JESS. It was just a quick Frenchie.

BILLY. He smells like gerbils.

JESS. He lives in a pet shop.

BILLY. You can do better.

JESS. I think this supervisor at Woolworths fancies me. Jason. He's thirty but he acts dead young.

BILLY. Thirty?

JESS. He's a DJ at the St George. I've started this thing. Flab to Flat in Thirty Days. It was in my mum's *Woman's Own*. It's clearing my skin up as well.

BILLY. How long you been doing it?

JESS. Two days. Mum says if I actually finish it, she'll take me to Tammy Girl and we can have a whole *Pretty Woman* montage thing.

Sound of the school bell.

Meet you at the gates after last period yeah?

BILLY. Oh, by the way, Miss Riley says next school play is *Romeo and Juliet*.

JESS. Shakespeare?! Ugh.

BILLY. And she said she's got an idea of who she wants to cast… (*He gestures that it's the two of them.*)

JESS. And you're mentioning this now?!

BILLY. But I'll tell her you hate Shakespeare.

JESS. Can I just shock you? I actually love him.

Scene Seven

Private Rehearsal – 1996, Sixteen

They're excited. Having fun. They are both competent, even good at the Shakespeare.

JESS. 'Then, window, let day in, and let life out.'

BILLY. 'Farewell, farewell! One kiss, and I'll descend.'

JESS. We're not doing the kiss yet.

BILLY. We've got to do it sometime.

JESS. It gets worse. It says 'he goeth down'

BILLY. Down the bush

JESS. 'ello!

BILLY. The rose bush thing, the trellis – carry on.

JESS. 'Art thou gone so? Love, lord, ay, husband, friend!'

BILLY. Are you having a stroke?

JESS. 'I must hear from thee every day in the hour'

BILLY. Typecast

She raises her middle finger while continuing as Juliet.

JESS. 'For in a minute there are many days
    O, by this count I shall be much in years
    Ere I again behold my Romeo!'

BILLY. 'Farewell!'

JESS. Don't look into my eyes, look here, in case we laugh.

BILLY. We won't laugh, we'll be in the moment.

JESS. Alright Stanislavski. I'm getting my hair cut on Saturday.
    I'm gonna get the 'Rachel Cut'.

BILLY. Have you asked Miss Riley?

JESS. No.

BILLY. It's not very Juliet.

JESS. Pretty sure Romeo wasn't a ginger little John Major but
    we work with what we've got. Right! Let's do it again, no
    messing.

BILLY. With the kiss.

JESS. Fine, but just lips. I don't even want to know you've got
    a tongue in your head.

BILLY. Ready?

They do this bit really beautifully.

JESS. 'Then, window, let day in, and let life out.'

BILLY. 'Farewell, farewell! One kiss, and I'll descend.'

JESS braces for the kiss, expecting it to be awful, but actually it's fine – the final hurdle to smashing the school play.

JESS. Oh my God, we're gonna fucking nail this.

Scene Eight

House Party – 1997, Sixteen

JESS is throwing a house party but has disappeared. BILLY is bursting with news when he finds her.

BILLY. Someone's been sick in your brother's bed.

JESS. What?

BILLY. And Lee Robertson's smoking weed on the stairs.

JESS. What the fuck is he doing here?

BILLY. Kelly let him in. And ten of his mates. He just asked me if Beautiful South is opera. Then he put a spliff out on the carpet. There's a black hole. Where the hell have you been?

JESS. In the garden.

BILLY. You can't just disappear from your own house party, Jess. Why you acting weird?

JESS. Ashley Timms has asked me to go upstairs.

BILLY. Wow.

Beat.

What about your 'boyfriend'?

JESS. Jason? He's a weirdo. What the hell's a thirty-year-old doing with a sixteen-year-old anyway?

BILLY. Thought you said he looked like Patrick Swayze in *Ghost*.

JESS. Yeah. Dead.

BILLY. So, you gonna go then?

JESS. Is that alright?

BILLY. Why you asking me?

Beat.

Look, I'll keep an eye on everything down here. If you want to…

JESS. Really?

BILLY. It's up to you.

Beat.

Scene Nine

Drunk – 1997, Sixteen

In the park. BILLY's drunk.

JESS. Billy, what you doing? Everyone's looking.

BILLY. Leave me alone.

JESS. Get up off the grass and give me that vodka.

BILLY. No.

JESS. Everyone's talking about us.

BILLY. Why?

JESS. Saying we've fallen out and that's why you're hammered.

BILLY. That's not why.

JESS (*quietly, just between them*). Ashley Timms was going out with Laura Robson the whole time anyway. So *she* fucking hates me now. And he told Tim Rose I'm a weird kisser. And that I smell. And that my thighs rub together. So

BILLY. Nobody loves me, Jess.

JESS. What? Oh come on.

BILLY. Everyone just laughs at me.

JESS. Because you're drunk and probably lying in dog shit.

BILLY. Tell me who loves me.

JESS. Billy, get up, please

BILLY. Tell me.

JESS. Your mum loves you.

BILLY. Wrong. She told me.

JESS. When?

BILLY. I don't know.

JESS. Right. Stop being such a drama queen. (*Reluctantly, because he won't get up.*) I love you.

BILLY. You don't know me.

JESS. God, are you joking. I spend every miserable moment with you. And if I have to listen to any more of your shit. Stop attention seeking, Billy. Everyone's looking and laughing at us. Get your arse off that muddy grass and let's go home.

Scene Ten

Grass – 1997, Sixteen

BILLY. Yours looks exactly the same.

JESS. Says on the bottle one shade lighter every thirty minutes.

BILLY. What have you packed?

JESS. Three pairs of shoes

BILLY. Three?

JESS. One for walking, one for indoors and one for dinner.

BILLY. We're going youth hostelling in Derbyshire!

JESS. Don't wanna be wearing walking boots if we meet anyone fit.

BILLY. I've only got these.

JESS. Good luck.

BILLY. God it's boiling. Three months of freedom. No more double science, with Tripod. Ever. Let that sink in.

JESS. No more maths with Barry Manilow and his light-up fucking board rubber.

BILLY. And when we go back, two whole years of Theatre Studies with Miss Riley.

JESS. We're gonna rule that drama block. The *Romeo and Juliet* posters are still everywhere.

BILLY. I put superglue on two of them.

JESS. Billy!!!

BILLY. It's like a reward for surviving.

JESS. I do love you, y'know.

Beat.

BILLY. Is it looking any lighter? (*Meaning his hair.*) I wanna be Brad from *Neighbours* by teatime.

JESS. Nah. Your freckles are going mental though.

BILLY. Great.

JESS. What shall we do while we wait?

BILLY. 'I Know Him So Well'. Bagsy I'm Elaine.

JESS. Why are you Elaine?

BILLY. Because I want to do that bit – (*He sings – a bit over the top.*) 'Looking back I could have played things…'

JESS. Not like – (*She sings – very over the top.*) 'LOOKING BACK I COULD HAVE…' You only want to be Elaine cos she starts.

BILLY. No. You look like Barbara Dickson, anyway – the nose – so it suits you.

JESS. You look like Elaine Paige fucked Boris Becker and gave birth way too early.

BILLY. Fucking hell, Jess!

They crack up laughing.

JESS. I'm wetting myself. Wait. I'll get some ice pops. Don't start without me.

Scene Eleven

NYMT – 1998, Seventeen

In the drama block, eating lunch.

BILLY. I had sex with Emily

JESS. Emily Parks? When?

BILLY. Yesterday

JESS. Oh my God. *After* her solo interpretative dance to 'Purple Rain'?

BILLY. That was classic.

JESS. It was weird.

BILLY. We had sex like Vivian and Edward on the piano.

JESS. What? Wait, what piano?

BILLY. Well, it was actually the Bontempi organ in the back room, and it gave way after about two seconds, fuck off

JESS. Oh my God! It was you two broke that?

BILLY. Shhhh.

JESS. So, are you going out with her now?

BILLY. Sort of. We're going to the NYMT auditions together.

JESS. Stop calling it NYMT, you're not in it yet.

BILLY. It's tomorrow in Birmingham.

JESS. I know.

BILLY. You should have applied.

JESS. I hate auditions.

BILLY. Why?

JESS. Don't wanna stand in the middle of a big room while posh people judge me. Fuck that.

BILLY. Well, you'll never go to drama school then.

JESS. You said you have to sit naked in a circle at drama school.

BILLY. They need to know you can be vulnerable.

JESS. I'm never gonna do that. Anyway, NYMT'll be full of wannabes and musical-theatre dweebs.

BILLY. You love musical theatre.

JESS. No, *you* love musical theatre.

BILLY. Jude Law was in it you know?

JESS. Jude Law?

BILLY. And Jonny Lee Miller.

JESS. He gives me the creeps with his white hair.

BILLY. You were all over *Trainspotting*.

JESS. I'm going out with Dwayne tomorrow anyway.

BILLY. Dwayne Chambers, why?

JESS. He asked me out, earlier.

BILLY. He's a total dick.

JESS. Fit though.

BILLY. In a Bill Sykes sort of way.

JESS. If you get in are you gonna use musical-theatre references
    for everything?

BILLY. Probably.
    Miss Riley was asking why you didn't apply.

JESS. What did you say?

BILLY. I said I didn't know.

JESS. Don't tell her I'm going out with Dwayne.

    Beat.

    So what song you gonna do?

BILLY. 'Empty Chairs at Empty Tables'.

JESS. Oh God. Don't do the acting eyes. Or that weird vibrato
    thing.

BILLY. Thanks for the pep talk.

Scene Twelve

Oliver – 1998, Seventeen

Jess's room.

JESS. Are you okay? You've been weird since that audition.

BILLY. Jess, I met someone.

JESS. Oh my god, Emily was literally there.

    BILLY *can't look at* JESS *for this bit.*

BILLY. His name's Oliver.

JESS. Oliver?

BILLY *finds* JESS*'s eyes.*

Right.
What happened?

BILLY. Mum was meant to drop us in Birmingham, but she couldn't, so we got the train and we were late. Emily had to go straight in, and I was just sitting there stressing out, and suddenly I noticed this boy looking at me.

JESS. Oliver?

BILLY. Yeah. We, kind of, locked eyes.

JESS. Oh my God. Then what?

BILLY. He just walked over and said, 'Are you okay?'

JESS. What does he look like?

BILLY. He's got blond tips and a face like Mark Owen.

JESS. Shit.

BILLY. I know. He's from Nottingham as well. He's in this drama group and he's already done *Rent*, and *Hair*. And he's so funny.

JESS. What did he say?

BILLY. He said, 'If I could be in any musical it'd be *Seven Brothers for Seven Brothers* because that would be sexy,' and I giggled like a

JESS. Freak?

BILLY. Yep. And he said I had a cute laugh. And I said, 'My girlfriend's dancing in the other room, we had sex on a piano'

JESS. You didn't.

BILLY. I did. And then he said we should swap numbers because this drama group needs new members.

JESS. Are *you* gonna ring him?

Beat.

BILLY. He rang me. We're meeting up on Saturday.

JESS. What!?

BILLY. Just to talk about this group.

JESS. Sure.

BILLY. It won't be anything else, he's proper boyband standard.

JESS. Billy, he asked for your number.

BILLY. I couldn't sleep last night. I just stared at the ceiling. I haven't eaten for two days.

JESS. What you gonna wear?

BILLY. I've already ironed my Ben Sherman shirt. It's three whole days away. What am I gonna do?

JESS. Pretend we're in New York.

She puts some music on.

BILLY. What?

JESS. It's what I do in Minsky's when I'm not drunk enough.

BILLY. Yeah but usually you are pretty drunk.

JESS *is dancing. Starts off pretty awkward but funny.*

JESS. Get it out your system.

BILLY. What are you doing? Oh my God. I need vodka.

JESS. Power up. Pretend you're in New York, Billy. You're on the podium. There's the Chrysler Building. Times Square. Central Park. The Empire State. Twin Towers. Broadway! Pretend you're on Broadway, Billy! (*Singing, rapping, riffing, taking the piss – have fun, whatever.*) 'Oliver! Oliver! Never before has a boy wanted more!'

BILLY. Shut up!

BILLY *is embarrassed and self-conscious but eventually joins in, cautious but happy. Potentially this morphs into a movement sequence to represent* BILLY*'s magical night with Oliver. He leaves the night and wanders back to* JESS*'s door.*

Scene Thirteen

Losing Oliver – 1998, Seventeen

BILLY *has been up almost all night.*

JESS. Tell me everything! Where did you meet?

BILLY. At the Left Lion. I was early, he was late.

JESS. What was he wearing?

BILLY. That Sweater Shop jumper *we* wanted. We went to this cool cinema, just for drinks, and then he invited me back to his house.

JESS. What the fuck?

BILLY. I know. We got the bus and all the way our bodies were touching, tiny little touches, and our hands were brushing when we went round corners.

JESS. Bet you kept wishing for corners.

BILLY. We walked up this big hill to his house. It's massive. Everything's cream and gold and it smelt like garlic bread in the oven. His mum and dad were there.

JESS. Ah, shit.

BILLY. They were sitting on this huge settee watching a film and they paused it and said, 'Ollie, there's a bottle of wine in the fridge if you and your friend want some.'

JESS. What the hell?!

BILLY. I know. We just walked upstairs with this wine. Oliver said, 'They won't mind if you stay over.'

JESS. Wow.

BILLY. Yeah, and the whole time I'm wondering if it's like, I'm gonna be sleeping on the floor, like I do here, y'know. I don't really know if I'm there as a mate or. And then he closes the door and he just walks over and starts, kissing me.

JESS. Oh my God.

BILLY. I know. He said – don't take the piss – he said he'd wanted to kiss me all day, and that I looked really good, I was like, 'no', and all this other stuff. And then, like, he's taking my clothes off and, yeah.

JESS. What was it like?

BILLY. Amazing.

It was kind of like a film, don't say a horror film

JESS. I didn't!!

BILLY. Like a film, only it was me and him.

JESS. And you left this morning?

BILLY. Yeah. Really early. And I just walked round town for ages because I can't go home. I'll have to sit eating tea and I just want to think about him. I borrowed his T-shirt last night and I forgot so I came home wearing it.

JESS. Oh my God, it's Ralph Lauren.

BILLY. It smells of CK One. What am I gonna do, Jess? I'm gonna go mad. I just want to see him.

JESS. Ring him.

BILLY. What?

JESS. Ring him and say you've got his T-shirt. Ask when you can bring it back.

BILLY. I can't.

JESS. Course you can. He did.

BILLY. I know but, it's a bit soon, it'll look a bit

JESS. It won't. I bet he's feeling the same.

BILLY. Do you think?

JESS. Billy, he took you back to his house. Ring him, now

BILLY. Now?

JESS. Before you talk yourself out of it.

BILLY *pulls a piece of paper from his pocket with Oliver's number written on it – six digits.*

BILLY. You can't listen.

JESS. I won't.

BILLY *is hesitant,* JESS *grabs the paper from his hand.*

Give me that number.

JESS *dials.*

BILLY. Jess! Oh my God. Go in the other room.

JESS. I will.

Ringtone. JESS *is hovering.*

BILLY. Oh, hello, it's Billy, Oliver's friend.

Fine thank you.

JESS *starts jumping around trying to contain herself.* BILLY *gesticulates wildly for her to go away.*

Is Oliver there?

Thank you.

BILLY *mouths 'fuck off' to* JESS. *She appears to go out the door.* BILLY *turns his back and doesn't notice she is still hovering.*

Oh, hi Oliver, it's Billy. Hi.

No, everything's fine. I just completely forgot I went home wearing your T-shirt.

Oh no, I can't do that, it's Ralph Lauren. I could come back into town and

Oh, okay then. Thank you. Anyway, I just wondered if you want to

Oh.

Right.

No. That's cool. Course. No I didn't think. It's fine. Course we can be friends, yeah. I've got a girlfriend, so.

Okay. Oh course, I'm definitely coming to the drama group. Totally. I'll, see you then.

Yeah. Bye.

JESS. Billy?

BILLY. He's got a boyfriend, so

JESS. What?

BILLY. Yeah, course he has. Look at him. I didn't think, it was nothing, just

JESS. No.

BILLY. It's fine. He says I can keep the T-shirt. Must think I'm a right charity case. God, I shouldn't have rung him, I look like a right

JESS. No.

BILLY. You shouldn't have made me call him, Jess. I knew it. As if he's going to…

JESS. I'm sorry.

BILLY. Forget it.

Beat.

JESS. What about Emily?

BILLY. I'm gay Jess.

JESS. I know.

Beat.

You can get in my bed for a bit, if you want. I won't bug you.

BILLY. Okay.

BILLY *lies with his back to* JESS. *He is completely devastated and humiliated.*

JESS. Please don't have a sad wank.

BILLY *isn't laughing.*

Scene Fourteen

Final Summer – 1999, Eighteen

End of the sixth-form summer ball. They've won a trophy.
BILLY is holding a bottle of Malibu. They're sharing a
cigarette. Maybe they pour Malibu into the trophy and drink
from that.

JESS. Why don't I keep it until Christmas then you take it. I'm
    going in February anyway and it won't fit in my backpack.

BILLY. 'Most Likely to be Famous.' Jessica Johnson and Billy
    Moss.

JESS. You should have won it. You're going to sit naked in a
    circle at drama school.

BILLY. Yeah, but you were amazing in the last play.

JESS. That Malibu's sending you weird.

BILLY. Ashley Timms looked fit in that suit.

JESS. He looked like Dawson at prom, God damn it. Dawson or
    Pacey?

BILLY. Pacey. Obviously.

JESS. Dawson's got nice arms but parental disappointment
    from your boyfriend is

BILLY. Definitely not the thing.
    When do you start looking for a job?

JESS. I'm signing up to this agency. They find you temp work
    in offices and stuff.

BILLY. You gonna click around in stilettoes and big glasses?

JESS. Yeah, black Wonderbra, white shirt. I'm planning a fully
    obsessive love affair before I go to Australia.

BILLY. You can still change your mind, y'know? On the
    English degree. You've got a year before you start.

JESS. Why would I?

BILLY. I just couldn't imagine giving up on acting.

JESS. Do you know how many actors there are already? Really good ones?

BILLY. I got in, didn't I?

JESS. It's alright for you, you don't have to pay fees.

BILLY. Yeah, lucky me with my single parent. She'd pay to get rid of me anyway.

JESS. She'll miss you like mad.

BILLY. She's already said my room's gonna be an entertainment hub. She's gonna put her midi hi-fi and her dildos in there.

JESS. Billy!

BILLY. Simon's round pretty much all the time now.

JESS. Is he still marinating in Lynx Africa?

BILLY. He was telling me the other day *he* knows a man who trained to be an actor who now sells old taxidermy from a bungalow in Stapleford. September can't come soon enough.

Beat.

JESS. Do you think things'll change?

BILLY. Do you?

Beat.

JESS. Don't start acting all different, doing those big intense eyes or speaking like Stephen Fry.

BILLY. As if.

JESS. Bet you never come home.

BILLY. Are you trying to tell me you'll miss me?

JESS *looks at* BILLY. *It could be a beautiful moment, but…*

JESS. Have you got foundation on?

BILLY. What. No.

JESS. Oh my God you have. Can see your sweat streaks.

BILLY. Fuck off. It's tinted moisturiser.

'Never Forget' by Take That starts playing in the distance.

JESS. Shhh, Mr Hallam's playing 'Never Forget'! Come on.

BILLY. Wait. I've got one photo left.

BILLY *pulls out a disposable camera and they hold it above them to get an old-skool selfie.*

PART TWO

ADULTHOOD

Scene Fifteen

New Job – 2002, Twenty-Two

JESS *is hiding at work to take a call from* BILLY.

JESS. Billy! Where you been?

BILLY. I got a job

JESS. That audition you went for?

BILLY. That was ages ago. I knew I wouldn't get that.

JESS. Sorry. What then?

BILLY. I'm going to be assistant to Rosine Mitchell.

JESS. Who?

BILLY. One of the biggest showbiz agents in London. She looks after the best actors. Name one.

JESS. Tom Cruise?

BILLY. No.

JESS. Brad Pitt?

BILLY. Fucking 'ell Jess, Emma Thompson? Hugh Grant? Basically everyone.

JESS. Wow, so what will *you* do?

BILLY. I get to go out every night watching theatre, for free, looking for new people to sign, and I'll help Rosine look after existing clients. And if it all goes well, I start to build my own list.

JESS. That's so cool

BILLY. Yeah, I'm going to *Celebrity Big Brother* next week.

JESS. No way!

BILLY. Yep, and I've got two West End press nights in my diary and a red-carpet event in Leicester Square.

JESS. Wow!

BILLY. I know.

JESS. What about acting though?

BILLY. I was deluded.

JESS. What?

BILLY. I'm not even that good.

JESS. You are.

BILLY. You never thought I was that good.

JESS. Miss Riley did.

BILLY. Yeah, well, mentioning Miss Riley's name in an audition weirdly doesn't get you anywhere. Anyway, two years in London watching everyone going for the same thing. I've maxed out two credit cards, Jess.

JESS. You could do it on the side, maybe.

BILLY. It doesn't work like that.

JESS. I'm just saying, don't give up on the dream.

BILLY. Come on, Jess. You're shacked up and working in communications for the County Council.

JESS. It's creative. I'm using my English degree.

BILLY. Can't you just be happy for me?

JESS. I am.

BILLY. I'll be hanging out with famous people, seeing all the shows, this *is* the dream!

JESS. It's amazing.

Scene Sixteen

Elton – 2004, Twenty-Four

BILLY *calls* JESS. *It's the middle of the night, she is knackered, he is drunk. At first, she's worried.*

JESS. Billy! Are you okay?

BILLY. What you doing?

JESS. I was in bed.

BILLY. You're always in bed.

JESS. It's 2 a.m. On a Tuesday.

BILLY. Where's your fiancé?

JESS. Paul *was* asleep. What's that noise?

BILLY. Guess where I am? (*Sings/blasts.*) *'Hold me close I'm a tiny dancer!'*

JESS. You're off your head.

BILLY. That's a clue.

JESS. Elton John's house.

BILLY. I'm sitting on his gold toilet.

JESS. You're in Elton John's bathroom?!

BILLY. One of. Jake Shears has been flirting with me all night. He's actually quite hot in real life.

JESS. Who's Jake Shears?

BILLY. Come on! Crawl out from under your Midlands rock, Jess. (*Sings.*) *'Do it! Take your Mama'*

JESS. Alright. Enjoy! (*Fuck off!*)

BILLY. Where *you* going?

JESS. Bed. Work's crazy.

BILLY. Council AGM waits for no man.

JESS. It's the middle of the night. Again. Last month you called me from Geri Halliwell's limo. Then Patsy Kensit's wet room.

BILLY. So sorry to interrupt the child-bride's suburban bubble.

JESS. I auditioned for a play last week.

BILLY. What? How come?

JESS. It's a community production.

BILLY. Oh right.

JESS (*from his reaction*). *That's* why I didn't tell you.

BILLY. If that's what you wanna do.

JESS. Anyway, I got the main part. I found out today.

BILLY. What is it? Maria von Trapp?

JESS. It's a new play, with songs, written by the director. I'm freaking out a bit.

BILLY. Why?

JESS. I haven't been on stage since school.

BILLY. It's amdram, love. No one'll expect it to be good.

JESS. We did this two-day audition thing, acting and singing. It was

BILLY. What?

JESS. Like a feeling I forgot. They've brought this amazing guy in to write and direct it. Kieran McCafferty. Do you know him?

BILLY. Never heard of him.

JESS. He's brilliant, Billy. Honestly, so smart. And hilarious. He had me in fits.

BILLY. Oh God, no. Cliché number one.

JESS. What?

BILLY. Actress falls for director.

JESS. I haven't fallen for him. Fuck off, Billy. I'm engaged.

BILLY. Alright.

JESS. Will you come and see it?

BILLY. What?

JESS. Mum's gonna get a big crowd together. Everyone'd love to see you.

BILLY. Oh don't make me. I already have to watch way too many actual shows.

JESS. I came to all your shows!

BILLY. I was at drama school. Bit different. I'm an agent

JESS. Assistant.

BILLY. Everyone'll be sidling up to me after – it's so gross.

You don't want me there, anyway

JESS. Yeah. It's embarrassing. I'll probably look like a

BILLY. Oh God (*Sound of knocking on the door.*)

JESS. What?

BILLY. Someone's just pushed a pill under the door. (*Shouting through the door.*) Nice!

I've got to… (*Squeal. Loads of raucous laughter.*)

Phone goes dead.

Scene Seventeen

Director – 2005, Twenty-Five

JESS *calls Billy's landline in London.* BILLY *is in the room but doesn't pick up.*

Answerphone message: Hi, it's Billy, I'm not home right now so please leave a message and I'll get back to you.

JESS. Billy. Where are you? Some stuff's happened. You know you said it sounded like I was in love with the director of the

community play and I went mad? Well, you were right. He
sent me a card on the last night and he said 'the intensity of
my performance' blew him away. I know. And after the show
I messaged him because he was back in London and we
just started texting for hours. It was like, electric. And Paul
asked who I was messaging and I just said, 'I can't marry
you.' Just rushed out my mouth like that. And his face, I'll
never forget it. He went mad. And I left, that night. Mum
was furious. But I was just obsessed. We arranged to meet,
in London. Yesterday. It was boiling. I got off the Tube and
I was waiting for the lift but it was crowded so I took the
stairs, so many stairs, and when I got outside, he said, 'Wow,
you look hot,' and, Billy, I said, 'Thanks!' and he said, 'No,
I mean, you're sweating.' And he laughed, not nasty, but.
He bought me a CD, because there's this amazing new song
and we both heard it on the radio at the exact same time and
text each other. It's called 'You're Beautiful' by a new singer
called James Blunt, do you know it? Course you do, you
probably know him. He took me down to the river and loads
of people were lying on the grass and kissing and it was,
romantic, really, but like, awkward. And, there's this other
thing. Oh God. I'm only saying this because it's you. He had
a wife who died. And they wrote this book together when she
was sick. About their love. This beautiful book. And I read
it three times, because, I'm a psycho like that. She was this
brilliant writer and artist and she had this incredible look.
And as we walked down Southbank it felt like she was there
behind me, the whole time. And twice I saw people with hair
like she had, in the photos, and I nearly said, 'She reminds
me of your dead wife.' What the fuck is wrong with me,
Billy? We held hands and he showed me so much but the
whole time I just felt, like, out of place really. But we kissed.
And it was good. I wanted it to be good. We didn't have that
much, he asked me what my favourite Cronenberg movie is,
and I said I don't know who that is, and his face, Billy. I just
felt so. He said, 'I could never love someone who's never
heard of Cronenberg.' It was a joke, but. And on the train
home, I just thought about his wife and the love they had,
and, oh God, I don't want to tell you this, because it makes

me want to die, but I'd had wine and I was all, but, I got
my laptop out and I wrote him a poem. I wrote him a poem
about how to get over his dead wife. I actually wrote that he
shouldn't let the death of his wife define him. And I left Paul.
I left Paul. And Mum's so mad at me I have to lock myself in
the toilet to cry. I can't talk to anyone.

BILLY *picks up.*

Billy?

BILLY. Did you send it?

JESS. Yeah.

BILLY. What did he say?

JESS. He said, 'Wow. Well, thanks for that advice.'

BILLY. Oh love.

JESS. And then, this morning, he sent me this long message
    saying he never expected me to leave my fiancé and that he's
    in no position to start a relationship.

BILLY. What a dick.

JESS. I spent the last ten hours watching Cronenberg films.

BILLY. Oh Jess.

JESS. I fucking love Paul.

BILLY. I know.

JESS. But I never wanted to write poems about him.

BILLY. I actually love that you sent it.

JESS. Really?
    I can't stop writing stuff, Billy. It's pouring out of me. I don't
    know what to do with it.

BILLY. Maybe don't send him any more though.

JESS. Are you okay? You sound

BILLY. I broke up with Patrick.

JESS. What? Why?

BILLY. I wasn't very nice to him.

JESS. Oh Billy. Are you

BILLY. James Blunt's shit by the way.

JESS. Really?

BILLY. Come on, love.

Scene Eighteen

Edinburgh – 2010, Thirty

Edinburgh Festival. BILLY *is standing under a massive umbrella.* JESS *runs to join him.*

BILLY. Oh my God. You look like you walked through a car wash!

JESS. How the hell are you not drenched?

BILLY. My hotel's two minutes away. And I got a cab.

JESS. Johnny Big Bollocks.

BILLY. Is that what you're wearing?

JESS. We've been flyering all day.

BILLY. You're the writer, love.

JESS. It's all hands on deck.

BILLY. That's why you need an agent.

JESS. Yeah, do you know any?

BILLY. I don't deal with writers.

JESS. I know, it was

BILLY. Have you got anything to freshen up with?

JESS. Not really.

BILLY. You've got ten minutes till they open the doors. It's quite a swanky party.

JESS. Sorry, since when did we use the word 'swanky'?

BILLY. It's quite a big deal then. I'm partner now, I can't

JESS. No, I know. Sorry. We've been having a crazy time. We were up all night flyering famous people in Pleasance Courtyard.

BILLY. Oh God.

JESS. David Hasselhoff says he's definitely coming!

BILLY. Target audience.

JESS. The others are all back at the flat. Maybe I should

BILLY. It's a huge party. There'll be loads of producers in there.

JESS (*getting out a Thermos flask*). Do you want some?

BILLY. What is it?

JESS. Gin. I'd like to say Edinburgh Finest but it's Tesco Basics.

BILLY. I'm having a sober summer.

JESS. No way?

BILLY. I've got this incredible PT in London but I can call him whenever.

JESS. God, don't. I've been living off Greggs for a week. I feel like I'm made of sausage rolls.

BILLY. Remind me to send you this *Men's Health* article about pastry.

JESS. I'll make a note. So?

BILLY. What?

JESS. Did you, have a good day?

BILLY. Apart from wanting to rip my own skin off managing fragile artists and watching 'promising' talent. Pressure's on to find something.

JESS. Did you, get the ticket I left for you or?

BILLY. Oh God, course I did. Sorry. Ridiculous day. Well done, love.

JESS. Yeah?

BILLY. Can totally feel you finding your voice.

JESS. Right.

BILLY. Some nice writing in there. Obviously, the cast could be stronger, you know that.

JESS. We've had some good reviews.

BILLY. National?

JESS. Not yet. Four stars in the *Edinburgh Post*. I know this is cringe but *Fest Magazine* said the writing's five star.

BILLY. Three stars overall though, right? It's a shame, that lead actor's really letting you down.

JESS. Ah shit. I told him you were in. He asked if I could

BILLY. You didn't?

JESS. He's probably just tired cos two-show day and then hours of flyering.

BILLY. Actors are so needy. Get on with it. Literally your job.

JESS. It's so hard up here though, isn't it?

BILLY. It's the game, I guess. It's tough playing small audiences.

JESS. How many were in?

BILLY. Maybe twelve.

JESS. Shit. Do you think you could

BILLY. I can't really recommend stuff that doesn't feature my clients. The message just gets a bit

JESS. Course

BILLY. Muddled, I know that sounds

JESS. No, honestly, don't worry.

I thought I might send the *Fest* review to Miss Riley.

BILLY. I've never known anyone as obsessed with nostalgia as you, Jess. Your writing's stuffed with it.

JESS. I think I'm gonna go back to the flat.

BILLY. What?

JESS. I look like a wet dog.

BILLY. There'll be loads of agents in there. Cara Moss is coming. She's a mate of mine.

JESS. From London Writer's Agency?

BILLY. Yeah.

Beat.

JESS. Let's catch up when you're home.

BILLY. Might not be till Christmas, now

JESS. Christmas? I saw your mum in Asda the other week. She said she never sees you.

BILLY. Well, she could come to London but, apparently, it's too crowded.

JESS. I'll come to London. Who knows I might get some meetings after this.

BILLY. I'll be in New York next month.

JESS. For work?

BILLY. Pleasure. With Jenny, from drama school.

JESS. I'd love to go to New York. Do you think I could come? I've still got some annual leave.

BILLY. Jenny doesn't really know you

JESS. I know Jenny

BILLY. Not that well though

JESS. You could ask her, see what she says

BILLY. It might be a bit awkward because then she'd feel

JESS. Yeah, sorry. I shouldn't have asked. I am different now though, I've changed, since Paul and the writing and

BILLY. I know. I'll be back in October.

JESS. I probably won't get any meetings anyway. This place is brutal, to be fair.

BILLY. I could maybe have a word with Cara.

JESS. Cara Moss?

BILLY. Yeah, if you send me your play, I could pass it on.

JESS. Really?

BILLY. Email it. Make sure it's formatted correctly.

JESS. Oh my God. Thank you. Right, you're going in. Have a wicked party.

BILLY. It's just work, love.

Scene Nineteen

Do You Think I'm Shit? – 2013, Thirty-Three

JESS *calls* BILLY. *She is in London. It is late afternoon and she has interrupted* BILLY *in the middle of a very busy, stressful day.*

BILLY. Jess, you okay? I'm in the middle of

JESS. I've just been signed!

BILLY. Oh my God!

JESS. I know! By Cara Moss.

BILLY. That's incredible.

JESS. You sent her my play after Edinburgh, remember?

BILLY. Course.

JESS. Three years ago.

BILLY. Everything takes time.

JESS. I know! I'm such an idiot. I've spent three years
    assuming she thought it was embarrassing cringe-level crap.

BILLY. Don't be silly.

JESS. Then I got an email last week inviting me in.

BILLY. That's brilliant.

JESS. Obviously we got chatting about you. She's a big fan.

BILLY. Ahhh.

JESS. But she said you never sent her my play.

BILLY. What?

JESS. She said she'd definitely have remembered.

BILLY. It was ages ago.

JESS. That's what I said. So, she searched her emails in front of
    me and nothing.

BILLY. I thought I'd sent it. I swear. I'm sending stuff out all
    the time

JESS. Do you think I'm shit?

BILLY. What?

JESS. Honestly, Billy?

BILLY. Come on.

JESS. Do you think I'm shit?

BILLY. Your stuff's not my taste

JESS. Why?

BILLY. That's not against you, it's just

JESS. Cara said my work's vital. She came to a scratch night I
    did. That's why she emailed me.

BILLY. There you go then. You don't need my approval.

JESS. I'm going to leave my job at the council.

BILLY. Really?

JESS. Yeah, so I can write. Mum and Dad said I can move back in with them.

BILLY. Seriously?

JESS. Do you think I'm stupid?

BILLY. Why do you care what I think? We barely see each other these days.

JESS. What are you talking about?

BILLY. Do you know how hard I'm working here to hold all this together?

JESS. Not really. From where I'm standing, you're out seeing shows every night, pissing fifty-quid bottles of wine up the wall and judging anything that breathes. What's happened to you, Billy? Do you remember when I stood outside stage door with you in Notts, freezing my arse off so you could get every single signature from the cast of *Joseph and His Technicolour Dreamcoat*? You were such a fucking dweeb.

BILLY *cries for a few seconds but he pulls it together as quickly as it started.*

Billy? Are you okay?

BILLY. I'm just shattered. I need some sleep.

JESS. Where are you?

BILLY. In town, I'm just, I'm

JESS. I can come and find you.

BILLY. I haven't got time. I'm

JESS. Forget it.

BILLY. I'm sorry, Jess. We'll sort something. Let's get a date in the diary.

JESS. Sure.

BILLY. Please.

JESS. Okay.

Scene Twenty

Stag Do – 2015, Thirty-Five

It's BILLY*'s stag do in London.*

JESS. Billy! I'm going to go back to my hotel

BILLY. It's only midnight.

JESS. It's been great, my first stag do! Ryan's amazing.

BILLY. Too good for me, you mean?

JESS. No.

BILLY. Stay for another mojito. I've barely seen you.

JESS. They're twenty quid.

BILLY. My treat.

JESS. I've booked a taxi.

BILLY. Jenny says you've been telling school stories.

JESS. Sorry.

BILLY. No.

JESS. Can't believe her and Jay have been together fifteen
    years.

BILLY. They're like the mum and dad of the group.

JESS. Jay was telling me his best-man plans. He's got three
    spreadsheets.

BILLY. They've been like my safe place since drama school.

JESS. Right. That's good.

BILLY. I'm glad you came.

JESS. Are you?

BILLY. I'm sorry, I know everything's been, chaotic. I've been chaotic. Things have settled down. You need to come and stay. We still haven't met Joe properly.

JESS. Yeah, let's sort something.

BILLY. I want to ask you something, before you go.

JESS. What?

BILLY. Will you do a speech, at the wedding?

JESS. Me?

BILLY. Yeah. We're both asking a friend. You've known me longest. I was hoping you might write something.

JESS. I thought my stuff wasn't to your taste.

BILLY *recoils at the memory.*

God, I dunno, Billy.

BILLY. Why?

JESS. All those impressive people. I don't know what I'd write.

BILLY. Just anything.

JESS. I haven't really seen you that much. I might say the wrong thing.

BILLY. You won't.

JESS. I just told your work lot how I used to stalk that weird guy from the garden centre.

BILLY. Oh God.

JESS. Exactly. I don't want to fuck it up.

BILLY. You're award-winning playwright Jess Johnson.

JESS. No pressure, then.

BILLY. You don't have to. It was just an idea.

JESS. No, thank you. I'd love to. How you feeling about it all?

BILLY. I dunno. Nervous.

JESS. Why?

BILLY. All those people from all different parts of my life, in one room.

JESS. Worried us hometown imbreds'll ruin your image?

BILLY. It's not that at all.

JESS. You always get depressed when you're drunk, Billy. It'll be brilliant.

    BILLY *gets a photo out of his wallet. He shows it to* JESS.

    What's this? Oh my God, that's you.

BILLY. Yeah.

JESS. How old?

BILLY. Three?

JESS. You look like a little matchstick. Where's this come from?

BILLY. Ryan gave it me.

JESS. How?

BILLY. I told him I didn't have any photos of me as a kid so he contacted my mum. I know.

JESS. What?

BILLY. It's weird.

    They got on dead well, apparently.

    We haven't invited her yet. To the wedding.

JESS. What? Why?

BILLY. Dave's not really supportive of us.

JESS. Well, fuck him then, but you've got to invite her.

BILLY. That's what Ryan says.

JESS. Honestly. She'd be devastated.

BILLY. It's our day, Jess.

JESS. Yeah it is, but

She's your mum. I'll look after her.

Her phone buzzes.

Shit. My taxi's here. Sorry.

BILLY. They'll wait.

JESS. Yeah, with the meter running.

Her phone buzzes again. JESS *leaves in a hurry.*

Send me some dates.

BILLY. Will do.

Scene Twenty-One

Wedding Speech – 2015, Thirty-Five

JESS *is making a speech at Billy's wedding.*

JESS. Hi, everyone. For those I haven't met yet, I'm Billy's friend, Jess. When Billy asked me to say something, I must admit my first response wasn't 'I'd be honoured,' but more along the lines of, 'Oh shit, why me?'

Not because I don't know Billy. I do. I've known him a very long time. But because this room is frankly terrifying. No offence. I'm used to just saying stuff then wishing I hadn't. But I wanted to get this right, because, annoyingly, I care what Billy thinks. I've always cared. In the way you do when someone you grew up with becomes a kind of internal measuring point without ever asking to be.

Billy says I'm obsessed with nostalgia, so I don't want to dwell too much on the past. But my first memory of him is seven years old, with a pumpkin head – his body's grown slightly in solidarity – sitting poker straight in the chair next to mine. Me in school uniform, even though there was no uniform, with a severe fringe my mum had kindly cut for me, and a very spiky sense of humour.

I was drawn to Billy from day one, especially when, out on the playground he got a group of us to gather round while he sung 'Nothing's Gonna Stop Us Now' by Starship. I was quietly impressed but, much like Marty McFly's guitar solo, some of the other kids weren't ready for it.

We were inseparable for years, my family loved *him* more than *me*. There's still no one in my life like Billy. But I haven't been a big part of *his* life in London. I've watched in awe to be honest, never quite sure where to stand.

And then he met Ryan. The most beautiful man. Warm and kind and with that rare quality of making people feel they can be exactly who they are. And I saw Billy again.

Ryan and Billy, I'm so happy for you both. Me and Joe can't wait to hang out as married couples, getting fat and eating cheese. Here's to the next chapter. Ryan and Billy.

PART THREE

PARENTHOOD

Scene Twenty-Two

I'm Coming – 2018, Thirty-Eight

JESS *is in hospital.* BILLY *is calling from his car.*

BILLY. Love, I just got your messages, I'm so sorry, we were out and

JESS. It's okay

BILLY. Fuck. How you doing?

JESS. Not good

BILLY. Where are you?

JESS. In the corridor. He's having the operation. I'm just, kind of

BILLY. Okay. (*Decisive.*) I'm in the car.

JESS. Where?

BILLY. Just passing Luton. I'm driving up.

JESS. You're not allowed on the ward, no one's allowed on

BILLY. It's okay, I'll sit outside, I'll go to the Costa or whatever

JESS. I don't know what

BILLY. If you can't see me, it's fine. I just want to be there

JESS. Because you think he'll die?

BILLY. No. Because I want to see you.

JESS. I look horrible.

BILLY. It's me.

JESS. Exactly.
    I stink.

BILLY. I don't care, love.

JESS. You hate Costa.

BILLY. Don't worry about me. I just want to be nearby.

JESS. I love you.

BILLY. I love you so much. Hang on. I'm coming.

Scene Twenty-Three

Elliot – 2018, Thirty-Eight

In the hospital.

BILLY. I bought you something. I know presents might feel, I
    didn't know what

    She pulls out a blanket or a teddy with her son's name on it.

JESS. Thank you

    She tries not to cry.

BILLY. I'm sorry if, is it a bit

JESS. I've never seen his name written on anything. It's like
    confirmation he exists. (*Trying it out in her mouth.*) Elliot.

BILLY. He does. He's beautiful.

JESS. He's not though.

BILLY. Oh God, Jess, he is.

JESS. Don't show anyone that photo.

BILLY. He's a little part of you and Joe. It's amazing. I'm so
    proud of you.

JESS. Why?

BILLY. Because you did that.

JESS. I messed it up.

BILLY. Oh love. You didn't. It's not your fault.

JESS. It might be.

BILLY. How can it be your fault?

JESS. Because I didn't know how utterly brutal it would be.
I knew it would hurt but, I thought it would just sort of
happen. And when it didn't, I was so fucking scared it's like
I gave up. And then I was panicking, all night, I was trying to
work out how I could get the fuck away. And in the morning,
he couldn't breathe. So that was me, wasn't it? That was
probably me.

BILLY. Oh Jess. Please be kind to yourself

Beat.

JESS. When you said you were driving here it's like a little box
of bugs fell over in my body and they just started crawling
around my insides.

BILLY. Is that a good thing?

JESS. When you're here it's like I wake up completely. Like
all these little fibres in me get filled up with electricity. It's
like what's going on in there (*The ward.*) isn't real any more
because you're here and I'm fifteen and I kind of want to just
prod you and poke you and climb over you and crawl inside
you. Not in a weird way.

BILLY. No. I mean, that doesn't sound weird at all.

Beat.

JESS. Shall we just leave, now. Go to the canal and get totally
hammered.

BILLY. Yeah.

JESS. No, I mean it. Can we go in your car and get some vodka
and just lie on the grass and get obliterated? Please.

BILLY. Maybe not right now.

JESS. They say a traumatic birth and how the mother bonds can cause mental-health issues in teenage years. Did you know that? So basically I've fucked him up already.

BILLY. You can't pin anything on that. So many factors play into it. I've done so much reading.

JESS. Have you? God, course you have. Sorry. I didn't ask you about

BILLY. Don't think about me.

JESS. But how did it go? On, God, what day is it?

BILLY. It's all good.

JESS. Is it? Is everything finalised?

BILLY. Yeah. He's coming to live with us on the fifteenth.

JESS. Oh my God. That's, when is that?

BILLY. Three weeks and two days.

JESS. Billy. That's amazing. How do you feel?

BILLY. Good. I don't know. Excited.

JESS. What's his name? Can you tell me now?

BILLY. Richard.

JESS. Richard?

BILLY. We wouldn't choose it but.

JESS. Will you change it?

BILLY. No. It's his name and he'll be fourteen months. We want everything to be as stable as possible.

JESS. What's his story?

BILLY. Erm, if it's okay, we're not really telling people.

JESS. Right.

BILLY. We want it to be his story to tell. When he's old enough. Whatever he decides.

JESS. Oh. Okay.

> *Beat.*

I can't wait to meet him anyway.

BILLY. They'll be little pals.

JESS. Promise?

BILLY. Definitely.

> *Her phone buzzes.*

JESS. That's Joe. The baby's coming out of surgery. Elliot.

BILLY. Right.

JESS. I'd better

BILLY. It'll be okay, love. Let me know, as soon as you can.

JESS. Yeah.

BILLY. I'm just going to stay here for a few hours.

JESS. I've got to be with him, really

BILLY. No, I know,

JESS. I don't want to.

BILLY. You can do it, Jess. I'll be here. Just, if you need me.

JESS. Thank you.

Scene Twenty-Four

Modern Parenting – 2022, Forty-Two

On Facetime – JESS *and* BILLY *in their own houses.*

JESS. Elliot needs another appointment. They said his chest is
growing weird. Like a pigeon.

BILLY. I'm sure they didn't say that.

JESS. No but when I googled it, it said, 'Also known as Pigeon chest.'

BILLY. I went out with a man with pigeon chest.

JESS. Did you? When?

BILLY. After drama school. Just very briefly.

JESS. Why, because of his chest?

BILLY. No.

JESS. Did it gross you out?

BILLY. Not really.

JESS. Great. I mean there's no superheroes with pigeon chest, right? No one on *Love Island*'s got a chest like a common urban pest.

BILLY. Jess, he's doing so well. He's beautiful.

JESS. He gets out of breath when he runs for ten seconds. Four-year-olds aren't meant to stop. When he cries, I feel totally sick. It's telepathic, I swear. I'm trying to deliver this fucking draft and I'm completely blocked by this low-level panic.

BILLY. Is your mum still helping?

JESS. Yeah, she idolises him and thinks I'm neurotic.

BILLY. Did she say that?

JESS. She's thinking it. That's worse. She keeps quietly encouraging me to have another. Apparently, that'll help.

BILLY. What do you think?

JESS. I can't think of anything worse.

BILLY. It'll change, love. What does the doctor say about his chest?

JESS. Just watch and see for now.

BILLY. Couldn't you go private? Get a specialist.

JESS. With what?

BILLY. Prioritise it.

JESS. Over what?

BILLY. I don't know. Just it's important.

JESS. Yeah. I mean, we're trying to stay calm really. Because they said we won't know until he's seven.

BILLY. Maybe focus on practical things. Didn't the doctor say you should get him into a football club or rugby or whatever?

JESS. Kind of.

BILLY. I'm sure they did.

JESS. No, they did but he's just not interested.

BILLY. I know but he's four. You could maybe persuade him.

JESS. He's not easily manipulated.

BILLY. Not saying manipulate

JESS. No, I know. Just, he doesn't like sport. How's Little Richard? The child, not the incomparable rock and roll

BILLY. That joke's wearing a bit

JESS. Sorry.

BILLY. Yeah. He's seeing this woman

JESS. The one who does the brain-sensor stuff?

BILLY. No, another woman – she puts this thing in his ear that traces his heart rate while he's doing different activities so she can objectively assess stress, emotional states and behavioural responses.

JESS. So what does that mean?

BILLY. It just helps us understand what stresses him out, what helps him regulate.

JESS. He's great though, isn't he? I mean he's not struggling or anything.

BILLY. There's a few things.

JESS. Whenever I've seen him, he's amazing.

BILLY. Yeah, but, we see him all the time and you know when you just, you get to see the whole picture.

JESS. Of course. But, don't worry, it could just be normal five-year-old stuff.

BILLY. Yeah. It could.

JESS. It sounds like normal five-year-old stuff to me. But I'm not an expert

BILLY. No. Just, given his start and

JESS. Obviously, I don't really know about that.

BILLY. We just want to make sure we're doing everything we can.

JESS. Totally. How much is it?

BILLY. What?

JESS. The ear thing, heart rate?

BILLY. It's expensive but I'm not sure there's anything more important to

JESS. Course. How's work?

BILLY. Full-on. It's a juggle. Ryan's in the New York office half the time.

JESS. Have you still got Mhari four days?

BILLY. Only eight till six. She's going away at Easter.

JESS. You could come up. I'll do them an egg hunt.

BILLY. Ah, I've got to work, holding it all together.

JESS. Could your mum come down and help?

BILLY. It's fine, we can cope.

I've got to do an online shop in a bit. I could have a look at some sports clubs near you if you

JESS. I know all the sports clubs. God. Literally the same as when we were kids.

BILLY. Well, you weren't exactly Sporty Spice

JESS. My brother and sister went to everything, my dad ran two football clubs, so I think I know what's

BILLY. Okay, just, I know you're busy

JESS. You're busy

BILLY. I've got some time this afternoon, there might be some new stuff

JESS. It's okay. I've looked. He doesn't like sports.

BILLY. Okay – well, listen, happy birthday. I was just calling to say that really.

Scene Twenty-Five

Surrogacy – 2022, Forty-Two

JESS *and* BILLY *are in the park watching Elliot and Richard.*

BILLY *is on a call.*

BILLY. No, I know. I said that would happen if they pushed him.

JESS. Elliot, be careful, stay on the small slide.

BILLY. No, it's okay, I'll go. Book me a flight for tomorrow morning. Fine.

He hangs up.

Fuck's sake.

JESS. You okay?

BILLY. Always a fucking drama with actors. Ryan's going to kill me.

(*To the kids.*) Richard, baby, Elliot wants to stay on the small slide.

JESS. Thanks

BILLY. You okay? Feels like you're doing better.

JESS. I finally asked for an extension on that draft. And I got Elliot into a gymnastics club.

BILLY. Oh fucking hell, well done, love. Can't wait to buy him a sequinned leotard.

Beat.

JESS. Little Richard's amazing y'know. He's so sweet with Elliot.

BILLY. Yeah, we're in a good place.

JESS. That's great.

Beat.

BILLY. We've actually been… thinking about having another.

JESS. Really? Wow. I wasn't sure you were still

BILLY. We always wanted two.

JESS. Yeah, just, obviously we always wanted two and then

BILLY. No, I know, love. I totally get that.

Beat.

JESS. So, are you on the adoption list or?

BILLY. Well, we thought it'd be easier second time round because it was so intrusive. But turns out if we want to do it again, we'd have to jump through just as many hoops.

JESS. Surely you've proven yourselves?

BILLY. Exactly. We're just not sure we want to go through all that again.

JESS. Right. So, what then?

BILLY. So, we're going to try and have our own instead.

JESS. Baby?

BILLY. Yeah. I think we're going to work with a surrogate. I mean, we are going to, that's what we're doing.

JESS. Wow. God. That's huge

BILLY. Yeah

JESS. That's amazing. So, how do you find a surrogate?

BILLY. The main place is actually Facebook.

JESS. Fucking 'ell, really?

BILLY. Yeah, but, well, you know Jenny?

JESS. Jenny? Course.

BILLY. Yeah, course. Well, amazingly, she's offered. It was actually her idea, we didn't ask, she just

JESS. Wow!

BILLY. Yeah.

JESS. God, it's such a huge thing to do for someone

BILLY. I know.

JESS. Physically and, all the anxiety

BILLY. Jenny's not really an anxious person

JESS. Until you've actually been through it, you can't even

BILLY. No, I know, but, she's got Molly and Jack, so

JESS. She had good pregnancies and births before, didn't she, so

BILLY. Yeah, all fine, all

    Beat.

JESS. It wouldn't be advisable for me to do it, to be honest, I mean, sorry

BILLY. God, no. I know, love.

    Beat.

JESS. So how did it all

BILLY. Funny story.

JESS. Is it?

BILLY. She actually offered at drama school

JESS. Drama school?

BILLY. She said I'd be a great dad and if I ever wanted kids of
my own someday she'd

JESS. She said that? When you were eighteen?

BILLY. We were drunk so I didn't really think, but then she
brought it up again at Christmas

JESS. Christmas?

BILLY. Yeah.

JESS. It's August.

BILLY. We weren't sure, but, yeah, Jay's completely on board.
Obviously, we're all really close so

JESS. It'll be like you're one big family in a way

BILLY. We've actually been talking about doing holidays
together

JESS. Right. So, what happens now?

BILLY. She's started taking the injections

JESS. Already?

BILLY. Yeah.

Beat.

JESS. You could have told me.

BILLY. No, I know, it wasn't

JESS. Wow. A little baby Billy.

BILLY. Ryan. We both agreed we want it to be his, biologically.
Just, Ryan was such a cute baby.

JESS. So, it won't actually be yours then?

BILLY. It'll be ours.

JESS. So, what about stuff like if she wants to keep it or

BILLY. It won't be her egg, she's just the host. Not *just*, God

JESS. Or if something goes wrong

BILLY. We've been having this mediation. You go through all the important stuff

JESS. What like if she dies?

BILLY. Jess!

JESS. Sorry, I mean there's so many unknowns

BILLY. Women give birth every day.

JESS. Oh, do they? Right.

BILLY. You know what I mean.

JESS. What about Richard? When he's older and realises he's not biologically related, but the baby is

BILLY. We'll just have to explain it. We'll take advice. You know how careful we are with everything.

JESS. Yeah, but, all the adopted babies that need a

BILLY. We've been through this, Jess. It's our decision. If Jenny hadn't offered, we wouldn't have even

JESS. That's not exactly a sound way to

BILLY. *You* didn't have to ask permission!

JESS. Look at me! Why would you ask a woman to do *this*?

BILLY. She's had two babies, she loved being pregnant, she offered.

JESS. Are you sure it's the baby you want or Jenny? One big happy family. Holidays together. You'll freak her out. I'd be freaked out.

BILLY. Fuck off, Jess.

JESS. Sorry. I'm sorry. I want to go home.

BILLY. Your train's not till tomorrow.

JESS. I think I'll ask Joe to come and get us.

BILLY. Oh, come on, please don't.

JESS. You could have told me.

BILLY. You've been struggling. I didn't want to upset you.

JESS. That's bullshit.

BILLY. It's not.

JESS. It makes me feel utterly fucking stupid. Do you know how, ugly, I feel. How totally fucking inadequate that I can't get my shit together enough to have another kid?

BILLY. You've been through so much.

JESS. It's not even that. I'm a mess. I can't even organise my *own* life. Joe wants another. Elliot asks me, 'Mummy, when will I have a brother or sister?' I can't do it. I hate myself. It's not even like my writing's going anywhere. It's embarrassing.

BILLY. Jess.

She is calling Joe.

JESS. No. I know. It's alright. I'll be alright. I just want to go home. I'm sorry. It's me. It's all me.

(*On the phone.*) Joe. Where are you?

Scene Twenty-Six

Blastocysts – 2022, Forty-Two

On the phone.

JESS. Billy. Hi. Sorry, it's been really busy here, but, I'm pretty sure this week's implantation week. I just want to say I'm thinking of you all. My God, Billy, I hope it goes really well. Oh, you're ringing me. Hello

BILLY. Hi, you were calling me

JESS. Yeah, I just wanted to say good luck.

BILLY. Jenny can't do it. So.

JESS. What?

BILLY. I don't blame her. It's fine.

JESS. But, why?

BILLY. A woman down here died in childbirth, it's been really big because she's a local nurse and, yeah, she had two other kids, so. It freaked Jenny out.

JESS. God, that's awful.

BILLY. Yeah, she's devastated, obviously. Feels terrible. I said she shouldn't. Just the fact she wanted to, y'know, that she went this far

JESS. Yeah.

BILLY. That's massive. That's everything.

JESS. Maybe she'll change her mind, in a few weeks or

BILLY. I don't think so.

JESS. You never know. Give her time, she might just

BILLY. She won't, Jess. It's been, yeah, intense, the mediation and, it brought up a lot and

JESS. Like what?

BILLY. Nothing, just, maybe it felt like a lot of, pressure. A lot of. For them, y'know, they've got their family and. So, yeah. You were right!

JESS. No. Billy. It's not like that. Are you okay?

BILLY. What other choice is there?

JESS. But, this is massive, this is like, months of planning and dreaming

BILLY. We're fine.

JESS. And money, so much money

BILLY. I don't care about the money.

JESS. So what are you gonna do now?

BILLY. Ryan wants to try Facebook.

JESS. Is that a good idea?

BILLY. We've got two top-grade blastocysts just sitting there.
    But I don't want to. That's not what I want.

JESS. Maybe take a bit of time off work. To figure it out.

BILLY. Leave us to it, Jess. We're two very capable grown-ups.

JESS. I know. You're amazing. I'm so fucking proud of you.
    Billy?

BILLY. I've got to go, Richard's shouting me.

Scene Twenty-Seven

Underground – 2023, Forty-Three

In London. Running for the Tube.

BILLY. Quick, jump on

JESS. It's too full.

BILLY. Come on

JESS. I'll wait.

BILLY. I'm not gonna go without you.

JESS. Just go.

BILLY. Fuck sake.
    We could have got on that one.

JESS. Yeah and suffocated with a stranger's dick in my back.

    I hate cramming in like that.

BILLY. You won't get to your meeting then.

JESS. I can't help it. Makes me feel panicky.

BILLY. God, you sound like

JESS. What? A provincial little fuck

BILLY. My mum.

JESS. Right.

I know you're mad at me.

BILLY. I just want to get to work. I'm knackered.

JESS. Well, you were at Glastonbury till Tuesday. With a seven-year-old.

BILLY. So what?

JESS. It's all a bit extra. The Instagram pictures with the big emoji face on Richard.

BILLY. We have to protect his identity.

JESS. Don't post any. Makes people feel like shit.

BILLY. What people?

JESS. Anyway. I thought he had sensory issues.

BILLY. He had ear defenders.

JESS. The other week you were getting him seen for sensory issues.

BILLY. Oh fuck off, Jess. We don't all have to bleed out on Instagram for attention. All those long rants about how hard it is to be a mother

JESS. They're not rants

BILLY. As if mothers have the monopoly on fucking parenting struggles

JESS. I'm just trying to connect with people.

BILLY. Well, you're doing the opposite, here.

JESS. At least it's real.

BILLY. People don't trust us to take care of kids. We're not allowed to bitch about it.

JESS. You can bitch to me.

BILLY. I'm a bit busy trying to live my life.

JESS. You don't even reply to my messages any more.

BILLY. They're not messages, they're monologues.

JESS. I thought that was fine. That used to be fine.

BILLY. You always say 'No need to reply', so I don't.

JESS. Just a thumbs-up.

BILLY. A thumbs-up would kill you.

JESS. A heart then. To say you're not going fucking insane.

BILLY. I'm trying to set boundaries.

JESS. Fucking 'boundaries'. Sounds like selfish twenty-first-century bollocks.

BILLY. Find a therapist.

JESS. I can't afford it.

BILLY. Prioritise it.

JESS. Above what? Food for Elliot?

BILLY. You're not some tortured working-class artist, Jess. It's a choice.

JESS. Is it

BILLY. Yeah, we've all had to make them. I'm not providing the therapy you can't afford because of how you choose to live your life.

JESS. I don't want therapy. I want my friend.

BILLY. You have this ability to just offload. Like this God-given right to be authentic. You have no idea what I've got going on.

JESS. Because you never tell me.

BILLY. What do you want from me, Jess? God, all you've got, all you've had. Why are you like this?

JESS. Like what?

BILLY. Exhausting. Messy, all the time. It's the same stuff, over and over. Why can't you sort your own shit out like I have to? Seriously! How the fuck does Joe cope?

JESS. I don't talk to Joe like I talk to you.

BILLY. Oh come on, as if I'm the 'chosen one'. Of all the manipulative, playground crap.

JESS. I'm worried about you, Billy.

BILLY. Why?

JESS. This isn't you.

BILLY. Looks exactly like me from where I'm standing.

JESS. Everything's crazy here. Come home for a bit. We can go out. Your mum can have Richard.

BILLY. No.

JESS. She misses you.

BILLY. As if.

JESS. I went round to see her.

BILLY. Why the fuck did you do that?

JESS. I feel sorry for her.

BILLY. Oh right! So you went round to drown your sorrows – two sad, failing mothers propping each other up.

JESS. Fuck you, Billy. You think you're better than all of us. No wonder Jenny freaked out. Terrified of being stuck with you for the rest of her life.

Billy! Are you okay?

BILLY. Don't you dare get on this fucking train with me.

JESS. Wait.

BILLY. I mean it. Leave me alone, Jess.

JESS. I'm scared, Billy. I'm sorry. Please.

Billy!

Scene Twenty-Eight

He's Okay – 2023, Forty-Three

Six weeks later.

JESS. Hi Billy, It's me, again, sorry. I spoke to Ryan the other
day. He might have told you. He said you're doing a bit
better. I was so relieved. I went down to the canal and I
just sat where we used to, all those Friday nights. Stupid
I know. I just wanted to be near you somehow. I'm sorry
about all the voicenotes. You don't need to listen. I know it's
probably selfish, surprise, surprise, but I didn't know what
to do. They're memories, spoiler alert. Not all good, trigger
warning. Just me trying to make sense of stuff, maybe delete
them. But. It's been six weeks and I wanted you to know that
I can't give up. I know I said, after, that day, that I'd leave
you alone. But. If I could just see you, one last time, I'll

Her phone rings, interrupting, she answers:

Ryan? How are you?

That's good. How's Billy?

Really? Are you sure he won't mind?

Okay. Thank you.

Thank you so much.

Scene Twenty-Nine

Breakdown – 2023, Forty-Three

BILLY *is in a bed in a private hospital. He has had a
breakdown but is now coming out the other side.*

JESS. Hi.

BILLY. Hi.

JESS. Ryan said it would be okay, I know you don't want to see
me.

BILLY. I never said that.

JESS. You look very regal, propped up there.

BILLY. Do I? Like an old queen?

JESS. You look good.

How you feeling?

BILLY. I'm scared they won't let me go home. Back to little
Richard. Because I'm mental.

JESS. You're not mental.

BILLY. He had a meltdown in the Co-op. A few months ago.
Because he didn't like the feel of his vest. And I felt this,
disgust, at his weakness. Just for a second, this absolute
shame. And then I started shaking. I couldn't stop. I felt like
I was dying. I don't know why I ever thought I was good
enough to do this. I mean, how dare I, really?

JESS. No. You're better than good enough, Billy.
After I had Elliot, I used to dream of escaping.

BILLY. I know.

JESS. I used to imagine I got sick, just so I could sleep. And in
my fucked-up little daydream, I'd be in hospital and you'd
arrive and crawl into bed beside me and we'd fall asleep
smiling, singing songs from school concerts, and then *you'd*
wake up and I'd be dead.

BILLY. That's nice.

JESS. Sorry. I'm only talking because I'm nervous

BILLY. Why?

JESS. Because. I feel like I've lost you.
Do you ever wonder

BILLY. What?

JESS. What it would be like, if
we'd never met?

BILLY. Yeah. I do.

JESS. Oh. And, what?

BILLY. And I think
I would have been lonely

JESS *sobs and pulls it back in.*

JESS. Sorry. It's relief, I think, it's relief.
Sorry. For the train, for causing this

BILLY. You didn't cause this.

JESS. For going to see your mum.

BILLY. You haven't told her about this, have you?

JESS. Course not.

BILLY. You think I should.

JESS. She'll probably want to look after you.

Beat.

BILLY. There's this, weird thing, it's not weird, this thing inside
me, that just wants, I think. Why does nobody really see me?

JESS. What am I missing, Billy?

Beat.

BILLY. She told me she wasn't capable of loving me. When I
was eight. She said she'd never be able to love me.

JESS. What?

BILLY. She said I was defective. When I was fifteen. In an
argument, but still. After I was beaten up, that night in Year
10 remember? And it was for being a 'dirty poof', by the
way.

JESS. You said he thought you were someone else.

BILLY. Because I was embarrassed. I got home and I stood in the middle of the carpet and I sobbed. I properly just broke. And she didn't do anything. She just stared at me.

JESS. You should have come to mine.

BILLY. I didn't want to go anywhere. I wanted my mum.

She used to whisper to people that I was a 'deep thinker'. She winked at them when I spoke. Once she got drunk and dared her boyfriend to ask me ten questions to guess if I was gay or not.

JESS. Fuck.

BILLY. There's so much stuff like that, loads of it. A thousand little cuts.

JESS. They're not little cuts, Billy.

BILLY. How utterly disgusting does a child have to be for their own mother to think those things about them?

JESS. No. It was her. It was about her.

BILLY. She stole any chance I had of feeling safe. That's the thing. As an adult, I get it. She's damaged. She's more insecure than me, for fuck's sake. But there's a really wounded little boy in me, that. Yeah. Poor little fucker, probably just broken forever now.

JESS. Not forever, Billy.

BILLY. I dunno.

JESS. I'm so sorry I didn't see it.

BILLY. It's not just you.

JESS. Yeah but it's me. We're family.

BILLY. I can't compare to your family. I always loved being with you all, but I felt this total envy too. Sometimes I wonder who I'd be if I was loved the way you were. I had to prove I was worth something. My whole life. If *you* failed at literally everything, you'd still be adored by all those people. God, the power of that. Must feel like some kind of magic. If

I let go of even a shred of what I've built, what am I? I never
wanted anyone to see *this*. Of course nobody loves me.

JESS. Do you honestly believe that?

BILLY. Yeah. It's okay.

JESS. So what do you think I'm doing? When I'm here loving
you?

BILLY. Loving a version of me. That I helped you create.

JESS. I love the bare fucking bones of you.

BILLY. I know you think you do.

JESS. I don't know who I am without you.

BILLY. You've always known.

JESS. You're the custodian of every version of me. I tell you
everything.

BILLY. Exactly.

JESS. I'll shut up.

BILLY. I don't want you to. I love the way you speak and say
how you feel. Just sometimes it's hard cos I don't understand
my own shit. Having your eyes on me is terrifying because
you see through most of it.

JESS. That's horrible.

BILLY. It's the opposite. You're the only constant in my whole
life, Jess. And when I let myself relax, it's actually the best
fucking feeling in the world.

JESS. I want you to tell me stuff. I want to understand. I'm
scared, but

BILLY. Why?

JESS. Because I think there's so many things I did wrong. I've
been going over *all* of them.

BILLY. I started listening to your voicenotes. Ryan had my
phone, while I was getting better, but

JESS. I'm so sorry. I know I'm too much.

BILLY. They're amazing. I wanted to reply. But. What if I start telling the truth and everything just, shatters?

JESS. It won't.

BILLY. You can't promise me that.

JESS. If we don't, aren't we just people who knew each other once? I don't think I could stand that.

BILLY. So what then?

JESS. I think, just, reply now. Tell me something I don't know.

BILLY. Like what?

JESS. Anything. If you want to. Only if…

Beat.

BILLY. Okay.

I guess, when I left home, for drama school, it was a relief. Finally. I could be myself. I felt free.

JESS. Of me?

BILLY. Partly, yeah. I'm

JESS. Don't say sorry. I get it.
What else?
Anything.

BILLY. Okay, this is, utterly pathetic. I loved Ashley Timms from the moment I met him.

I even got a boner in Year 5 assembly because I saw a bit of the skin on his back.

JESS. Year 5?

BILLY. Yeah.

JESS. I was so fucking insecure. I'm sorry.
I saw him the other day.

BILLY. Ashley?

JESS. Yeah, in little Tesco. I was in my pyjama bottoms with
    tiny fucking eyes.

BILLY. Obviously.

JESS. He said, 'Wow, I didn't expect you to be living in Long
    Eaton. I really thought you'd do something impressive.'

BILLY. Did you say, 'I'm an award-winning playwright'?

JESS. No. I was holding a box of Tampax. He lives in Dubai.

BILLY. Course he does.

JESS. He asked after you.

BILLY. Really? Did you tell him I'm clinically insane?

JESS. No. I told him you're amazing.

    Billy?

BILLY. What?

JESS. Do you really think I'm a failing mother?

BILLY. Of course I don't. Elliot is creative and clever and
    hilarious. And happy, Jess. He knows he's adored.

JESS. Okay.

    You said, before, about that night you got beaten up. What
    happened?

BILLY. You'll think I deserved it.

JESS. Never.

BILLY. Me and Lindsay, we did this stupid little dance, in the
    pub, just for a few seconds, that's why

JESS. You're allowed to dance, Billy.

    BILLY *is overcome.* JESS *goes to sit on the bed, then she
    lies beside him.*

    Here. Just relax. Close your eyes. It's gonna be okay.

    Hey, I went to a yoga class the other day. Oi! Don't laugh.
    It's part of my current obsession with being a better person.

It was in a cold church hall, and I couldn't do the poses properly. Obviously. Fuck off. I was actually thinking it was a complete waste of time. But then we got to the end and the woman lit candles and turned all the lights off and we had to lie down under thick blankets and she said, 'imagine you're walking into a garden, maybe it's a long path or a gate or a gap in a wall', and immediately I was in Mum and Dad's garden, our garden at home. And you were there, lying on the grass. It was so hot. It was GCSE year and we'd sprayed our hair with Sun-In, waiting for it to dry, and we were talking about what we were going to do after exams. Sixteen and an extra-long summer sprawling ahead of us, laughing like drains and stretching out in the sun with ice pops. I don't know what that yoga woman did but suddenly I was sobbing. And my whole body was just completely flooded with love for you.

Every time I get so stressed I can't breathe, I try to conjure that feeling, on the grass beside you, at Mum and Dad's. With the sun in our bones and those beautiful freckles all over your face.

Oi, if we fall asleep, don't you dare be dead when I wake up.

Scene Thirty

Billy's Voicenote – 2024, Forty-Four

BILLY *leaves* JESS *a voicenote.*

BILLY. Hiya ducky, it's me. Leaving you a really early message. I'm out in the garden, before Richard wakes up. It's a beautiful morning. I've been thinking about you ever such a lot. I had therapy again yesterday. It's helping. Heavy and hard work, but. Last night I went for a run and our play list came on and I burst into tears. I couldn't stop crying. But it's good. I've been making notes, on my phone, of all the

things I need to talk to you about. It still makes me nervous.
If I let you in and share my stuff, it's gonna come undone.
I told you at our stag do I was anxious about all the people
from different parts of my life in one room, but actually it
was about all those different parts of me, how I was going to
show up in that room with loads of people who all knew me
differently? But I think now, I'm starting to show up in most
rooms as the same person. That's the dream, anyway. I still
haven't seen mum. Maybe one day. But I'm listening to little
Billy for now, and I'm proud of myself. And I'm proud of
you. For following our dream of being an artist. I'm sorry
I've never said it. I can't wait to see you all next weekend.
Richard's already made a little bed on the floor for Elliot.
He's so excited. We all are. I love you so much. See you
soon.

A Nick Hern Book

Scenes from a Friendship first published in Great Britain as a paperback original in 2026 by Nick Hern Books Limited, The Glasshouse, 49a Goldhawk Road, London W12 8QP, in association with Nottingham Playhouse

Scenes from a Friendship copyright © 2026 Jane Upton

Jane Upton has asserted her right to be identified as the author of this work

Cover photography by Phil Crow; imagery by Tom Partridge.

Designed and typeset by Nick Hern Books, London
Printed in Great Britain by Mimeo Ltd, Huntingdon, Cambridgeshire PE29 6XX

A CIP catalogue record for this book is available from the British Library

ISBN 978 1 83904 592 9

www.nickhernbooks.co.uk/environmental-policy

Nick Hern Books' authorised representative in the EU is
Easy Access System Europe – Mustamäe tee 50, 10621 Tallinn, Estonia
email gpsr.requests@easproject.com